LUCY MICKLETHWAIT was born in Quetta, Pakistan, and as
a child in a military family she was brought up all over the world;
her parents eventually settled in Scotland. Together with Brigid Peppin
she wrote the *Dictionary of British Book Illustrators: The 20th Century*,
which won a Library Association Award in 1983. She is the author
of the highly successful I Spy series, which includes *Numbers in Art,*
An Alphabet of Art, Transport in Art, Shapes in Art and *Symbols in Art.*
Her other children's art books include *A Child's Book of Art,*
Spot a Cat and *Spot a Dog* – both winners of the Parents' Choice Award
in 1995, *A Child's Book of Play in Art* and *Discover Great Paintings.*
Other titles in the First Art Book series include *Colour a First Art Book*
and *Children a First Art Book*. Lucy lives in East London.

For Walter and Molly

Animals A First Art Book copyright © Frances Lincoln Limited 2004
Text copyright © Lucy Micklethwait 2004
The right of Lucy Micklethwait to be identified as the author of this work
has been asserted by her in accordance with the Copyright,
Designs and Patents Act, 1988 (United Kingdom).

First published in Great Britain and the USA in 2004 by
Frances Lincoln Children's Books,
4 Torriano Mews, Torriano Avenue, London NW5 2RZ
www.franceslincoln.com

Distributed in the USA by Publishers Group West

First paperback edition published in Great Britain in 2006
and in the USA in 2007.

British Library Cataloguing in Publication Data
available on request

ISBN 10: 1-84507-104-2
ISBN 13: 978-1-84507-104-2

Printed in China

1 3 5 7 9 8 6 4 2

Animals

A First Art Book

Lucy Micklethwait

F

FRANCES LINCOLN
CHILDREN'S BOOKS

Big and bold

elephant

rhinoceros

Bouncy

frog

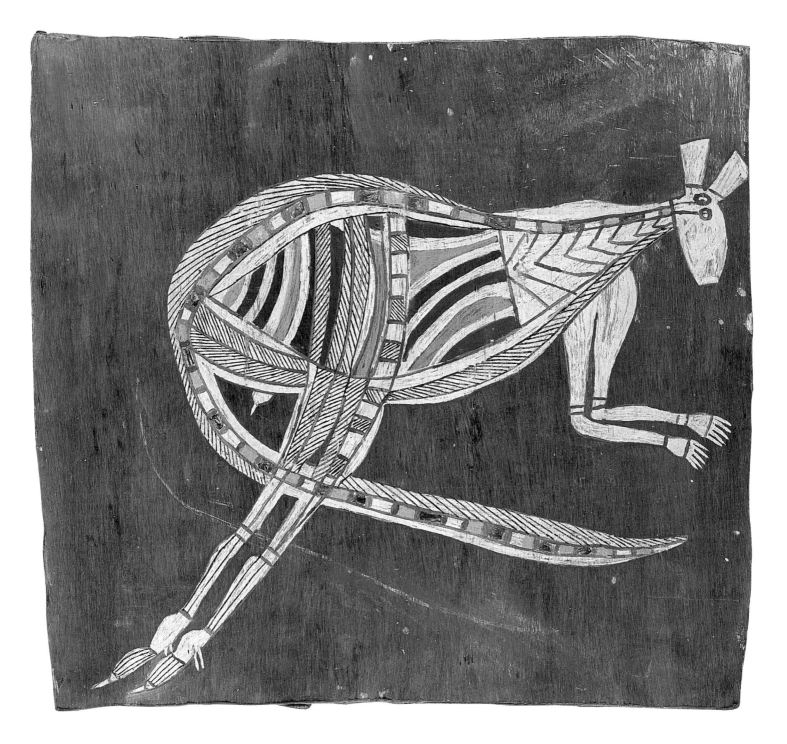

kangaroo

Spotty

leopards

giraffe

Stripy

zebra

tiger

Scaly

fish

crocodile

Furry

rabbits

squirrel

Feathery

cock and hen

parrot

Creepy crawly

stag beetle

butterfly, bugs and moths

Cuddly

dog

cat

Picture List

Big and bold

elephant
Prince Riding on an Elephant (16th century), Khem karan
The Metropolitan Museum of Art, Rogers Fund, 1925

rhinoceros
Black Rhinoceros from the *Endangered Species* portfolio
(1983), Andy Warhol (1928–1987)
Private Collection

Bouncy

frog
Frog, from the picture album *Meika Gafu* (1814),
Matsumoto Hoji
The British Museum, London

kangaroo
Kangaroo, Irvala (1903–1976)
National Museum of African and Oceanic Arts, Paris

Spotty

leopards
A Pair of Leopards (1845), William Huggins (1820–1884)
Private Collection

giraffe
The Nubian Giraffe (1827), Jacques-Laurent Agasse
(1767–1849)
The Royal Collection, Windsor

Stripy

zebra
Zebra (1763), George Stubbs (1724–1806)
Yale Center for British Art, USA, Paul Mellon Collection

tiger (also on Title Page)
Charger (1997), Kendra Haste (born 1971)
Private Collection

Scaly

fish
Carp (early 19th century), Katsushika Hokusai (1760–1849)
Musée Guimet, Paris

crocodile
Crocodile (19th century), detail from a Bengali scroll painting
The British Museum, London

Furry

rabbits
Rabbits, from *Kyōsai rakuga* (1881), Kawanabe Kyōsai
(1831–1889)
Rijksmuseum, Amsterdam

squirrel
Red Squirrel (1578), Hans Hoffmann (*c.* 1530–1591/2)
National Gallery of Art, Washington, Woodner Collection

Feathery

cock and hen
Cock and Hen (*c.* 1900), Yoshikuni
Private collection

parrot
A Parrot (17th century), circle of Peter Paul Rubens
(1577–1640)
Courtauld Institute Gallery, London

Creepy crawly

stag beetle
Stag Beetle (1505), Albrecht Dürer (1471–1528)
The J. Paul Getty Museum, Los Angeles

butterfly, bugs and moths
Study of Butterflies and Insects (*c.* 1655), Jan van Kessel I
(1626–1679)
National Gallery of Art, Washington, Gift of John Dimick

Cuddly

dog (also on Front Cover)
Little Stanley Sleeping (1987), David Hockney (born 1937)
Private Collection

cat
Julie Manet with Cat (1887), Auguste Renoir (1841–1919)
Musée d'Orsay, Paris

PHOTOGRAPHIC ACKNOWLEDGEMENTS
elephant: © 1988 The Metropolitan Museum of Art
rhinoceros: © Copyright The Andy Warhol Foundation for
the Visual Arts/ARS, NY and DACS, London 2004
Photograph © The Andy Warhol Foundation, Inc./
Art Resource, NY
frog: © The British Museum (Japanese 1979.0305.0.236)
kangaroo: © RMN – Gérard Blot
leopards: The Maas Gallery, London/Bridgeman Art Library
giraffe: The Royal Collection © 2004, Her Majesty Queen
Elizabeth II
zebra: Bridgeman Art Library
tiger: Artists for Nature Foundation, The Netherlands
fish: © RMN – Thierry Ollivier
crocodile: © The British Museum (OA 1955.10-8.095)
rabbits: © Rijksmuseum, Amsterdam
squirrel: © 2004 Board of Trustees, National Gallery of Art,
Washington
cock and hen: Private Collection
parrot: Bridgeman Art Library
stag-beetle: © The J. Paul Getty Museum
butterfly, bugs and moths: © 2004 Board of Trustees,
National Gallery of Art, Washington
dog: © David Hockney
cat: Bridgeman Art Library